Dedication

I dedicate this to Bill Lewis, my friend and theological sparring partner, and to all the honest seekers and doubters of our divided Church. You represent some of the very best of my beloved Protestant tradition. May the God and Father of our Lord Jesus Christ carry to completion the work of unity, love and faith He is doing in the earth by His Holy Spirit.

Acknowledgments

This book, like all God's creatures, is not the product of isolation. It was born of the love and support shared by a community of dear sisters and brothers, both Protestant and Catholic. Without them, it simply never would have been written. In particular, I would like to express my profound gratitude to the following persons:

— First and foremost, to God the Father, Son and Holy Spirit Whose Name I wish to glorify by this offering even as He showers glory on us through His incredible love.

— To my wife Janet, whose astounding capacity to love is a beacon of the Holy Spirit. Thank you for everything you are. I love you.

— To our dear sons, Luke and Matthew, the best boys in the world.

— To Sherry Weddell, for her unfailing and unique friendship, her incisive editorial acumen, and her tireless support during the mini-crises that periodically becloud me. You're the one who helped me see I could do it.

— To the Seattle Catholic Study Group and the Seattle Great Books Reading Group. You are comrades all and treasured friends.

— To Dan O'Neill, for his invaluable assistance and astonishing generosity.

— To Steven Greydanus, for his friendship, his fun letters, his insightful criticism and his peachy artwork. I owe you one!

This Is My Body:
An Evangelical Discovers
The Real Presence

Mark P. Shea

Christendom Press

Foreword

I have to read the kind of thing I write, so I have read many books of Catholic apologetics; also many autobiographical accounts of conversions to the Church; and a number of excellent books which do both (like Sheldon Vanauken's *A Severe Mercy*, and the accounts in *The New Catholics* and *Spiritual Journeys*. Mark Shea's *This Is My Body* stands out to me as much more readable, more interesting, and more passionately truth-seeking than most.

It is also delightfully clear, free from platitude, cliché, vagueness, and dullness. It is "a corking good *read*."

It is also beautifully and strongly *rational* — so much so that its arguments seem not just reasonable but unanswerable. I hope some first-rate Protestant theologian reads it and has the moxie to take up the debate. The ensuing dialog would be on a very high level, like Ronald Knox and Arnold Lunn.

Mr. Shea writes very much in the tradition of C. S. Lewis. He thinks and writes as clearly as an Englishman; yet, amazingly, he is an American.

Happily, he has chosen to write a short and specific book. It is not "scholarly research," nor is it "popularization," but the high-level in-betweenness so neglected since Lewis' day. Just enough time and space is spent on this one crucial dogma, the Eucharistic Real Presence, to do it Socratic, investigative justice. This is no shallow "survey" or summary; it is in depth. But it is also very clear. It is not written for or by "experts." (God save us from them!) If all Christian writers combined these two virtues — clarity and depth — as well as Mr. Shea does, we would see a great revival in our confused world.

— *Peter Kreeft*

Introduction

GERRY MATATICS

I speak around the country, and occasionally abroad, on a variety of theological topics, but my favorite talk, far and away, is "How the Bible Converted Me to Catholicism" (with a book by that title to be published by the time you read these words). Once when sharing my story as the guest on a radio show in L.A., a listener called in, identified himself as a fellow convert, and informed us that playing the tuba had been instrumental in *his* conversion. (He didn't actually use the word *instrumental*, but I couldn't resist.)

The show was running short of time, but I was so intrigued by his opening line that, at the risk of unnerving the station's big brass — not to mention finding myself playing second fiddle to what might turn out to be a more sensational story (visions of being upstaged and outsold by a book entitled "How the *Tuba* Converted Me to Catholicism" gave me a momentary spasm of panic), I asked him to elaborate.

The caller explained that in junior high school he had been sick the day the instruments were handed out for band class (which was mandatory). When he showed up the next day, the only one left was the huge, hulking horn nobody wanted. While his firends flitted home and back clutching a clarinet, packing a piccolo, or boasting a bassoon (in order to practice at home), he trudged to and fro twice a day cursing the inventor of the musical millstone that hung about his neck.

In the course of his toilsome twelve-block trek, he would frequently stop in the doorway of one of several churches which lined his route, in order to catch his breath and warm himself (it was winter, and Wisconsin). His moments of rest at the Methodist, Episcopal, Baptist, and Pentecostal waystations were without event, but the first time he paused inside the Catholic Church, he felt Something (Some*one*, he would learn later) he had not experienced elsewhere: a Presence. Investigating further and learning from the local priest the marvelous truth that Christ was *there* in the Blessed Sacrament, he began receiving instruction in the Catholic Faith and eventually rejoiced to join the Church that could give him That Which no other church could.

This little book testifies, in a somewhat different way, of that same Encounter and Discovery, and for that reason I am delighted to write an introduction to it. It belongs to a genre of which I am especially fond and which seems to be making a major comeback: the narrative of a soul's search for Truth, a search which can only successfully end in the Catholic Faith. John Henry Newman's *Apologia Pro Vita Sua*, G. K. Chesterton's *Autobiography*, Ronald Knox's *A Spiritual Aeneid*, Arnold Lunn's *Now I See*, as well as the ruminations of more recent converts (Malcolm Muggeridge, Walker Percy, Thomas Howard, Sheldon Vanauken, John Michael Talbot) were influences in my own conversion, and I cannot help but believe that this little book, while not a full-blown conversion story *per se* but nonetheless a real record of discovery, will light the way for other pilgrims' feet.

I am thrilled as well that Mr. Shea meets evangelical objectors to eucharistic truth on their own terms and turf by trying his case before the bar of the Bible itself, subjecting the Catholic contention to the searching scrutiny of Sacred Scripture (but then, what would you expect from an erstwhile evangelical?). The need to champion the biblical basis of Catholic beliefs is crucial in our day, especially in our (historically Protestant) American *milieu*. During my fourteen years as an evangelical Protestant I was convinced that Catholics were sorry souls with no scriptural support for their papist perversions. This perception persisted through years of advanced theological training at both the master's and doctoral level at two of the finest evangelical seminaries in the country. It was not until I was forced to actually read Catholic apologetical works (in an attempt to save a good friend from seminary and a fellow Presbyterian minister from throwing his soul away by converting to Catholicism) that I made the astounding discovery that the Bible, far from refuting Catholic dogma, actually *supported* it. I was shocked to find out that exegetical arguments could be made for everything I had formerly found ill-founded: the papacy, purgatory, prayers to the saints, sacred tradition, the seven sacraments, the sacrificial character of the mass, the immaculate conception, perpetual virginity, bodily assumption and maternal intercession of Mary — in short, the whole nine yards. Needless to say, I not only failed to dissuade my friend (the only failure in my life I don't regret for a moment), I ended up becoming convinced that to go on being a "Bible-believing Christian" I had absolutely no choice but to come, regardless of the cost and controversy, into the Church myself, which I did with my wife and children at the Easter Vigil service of 1986.

I have since founded **Biblical Foundations**, a nonprofit apologetics apostolate, to do full-time precisely the sort of thing Mr. Shea does so well in this book: demonstrate that the Catholic Faith *is* biblical Christianity. I am convinced that the 1990's could prove to be the decade of mass conversions (pun intended) among evangelicaldom to the Ancient Faith, if we can present the case for Catholicism in a way that is understandable and credible to that audience, and that means biblical proofs — by the truckload. God knows the Catholic Church in America, pale and anemic as it is, could desperately use a massive blood transfusion of what our separated brethren so often outpossess us in: a deep hunger for Scripture, an unshakable confidence in its total inerrancy (a confidence shared by the magisterium of the Catholic Church — see Leo XIII's encyclical *Providentissimus Deus: On the Study of Sacred Scripture*, or Pius XII's *Divino Afflante Spiritu: On the Promotion of Biblical Studies* — and those Catholics faithful to the magisterium's teaching, but painfully absent in most Catholic Scripture scholars in this age of apostasy), a commitment to teaching the Bible, preaching the Bible, memorizing the Bible, making the Bible come alive in their lives and the lives of their children. God bless them for their zeal! And God grant that they bring that zeal back to where it belongs, transplant it into its native soil, the Ancient and Apostolic Church, where it can grow to full flower, can renew and revive the Church, and can attract yet other evangelicals to their True Home.

This Is My Body:
An Evangelical Discovers
the Real Presence

"It's a flagrant violation of Scripture," asserted Bill, my Evangelical Protestant buddy. "To take this teaching seriously is tantamount to participating in human sacrifice. Besides, God forbids the eating of blood under both the Old and New Covenants. You can't reconcile it with God's Word."

We were speaking of that bulwark of Catholic faith, the doctrine of the Real Presence: that "in the nourishing sacrament of the Holy Eucharist, after the consecration of the bread and wine, our Lord Jesus Christ, True God and True Man" is present "under the appearances of those sensible things"[1] — in other words, that the bread and wine actually become the Body and Blood of Christ. In my friend's objections I heard echoes of my own Protestant past: that it is only a memorial; that the worship of the Eucharist as the actual

---

[1]Council of Trent, *Decree on the Most Holy Sacrament of the Eucharist*, I: Denzinger 874 (1636).

Body and Blood was idolatry and salvation by works —
"the Kingdom of God is not a matter of eating and
drinking, but of righteousness, peace and joy in the Holy
Spirit."[2]

Few things can raise the hackles of good
Evangelical Protestants like this unearthly teaching. For
a variety of reasons having to do with a certain
perception of Scripture and a particular cultural
framework, the Evangelical's reaction to it is one of
honest incredulity. Yet it is emphatically not, I think,
simply because he or she feels the doctrine is macabre.
No serious Evangelical weighs a doctrine by its
prettiness. If that were the case, the ancient warning of
"the worm that dieth not and the fire that is not
quenched,"[3] so repugnant to the gut and heart, would
have been scrapped long ago. Yet the existence of Hell is
nevertheless acknowledged — despite its horrific ugliness
— by millions of Evangelicals for the straightforward
reason that, whether they like it or not, Christ said it was
so.

The criterion for an Evangelical is the simple
question, "Is it biblical?" The Evangelical's incredulity
about the Real Presence arises from a conviction that,
surely, it is not. It *must* be medieval hocus-pocus[4]

---

[2]Romans 14:17. (All quotes are from the New
International Version unless otherwise noted.)

[3]Isaiah 66:24; Mark 9:47-48 among others.

[4]For you trivia buffs, "hocus pocus" is a corruption of

foisted on the church by fools who had forgotten their Bibles; pinheads with whom no angel ever danced.

I know this profound doubt well. My Christian roots (a fairly generic Evangelical/Charismatic/Non-Denominational mix) were formed in an atmosphere heavy with it. Where I came from, disbelief in the Eucharistic Real Presence had the character of a premise, not an argument. We spent very little energy trying to *disprove* it; the assumption was that this had been done long ago. Still, the Real Presence gradually began to attract my attention, particularly when I saw that great Christians such as Augustine, Francis of Assisi, Thomas Aquinas, G. K. Chesterton, Mother Teresa and a host of others have held this belief, not as unexamined cultural baggage, but as an integral part of their faith. The sacrament became mysteriously fascinating to me, like a locked room in an old family estate. Everyone said there was nothing in there; then one day I looked for myself.

Beginning with the question "Is the Eucharistic Real Presence *un*biblical?," I was drawn to re-examine my assumptions one by one. In doing so, I discovered that instead of dissuading me from the ancient teaching, they had the peculiar habit of nudging me closer to

---

"Hoc est enim corpus meum," the words of consecration prayed in the Latin Mass through which, according to Catholic belief, God changes the bread and wine into the Body and Blood of Christ. It means in English, "This is my body" (Matthew 26:26).

believing it. What was more, I was surprised to find a number of other brothers and sisters in Christ walking the same bumpy road with me. In the end, I decided that it might be worthwhile to contribute what little light I had to the cause. This, then, is a spiritual journal written to help make straight the path for other pilgrims. As a layman, I do not pretend to be giving a comprehensive treatise on the Blessed Sacrament. My goal is to clear a path. It is the reader's option to walk that path to a fuller understanding than mine.

Considering the Alternatives

I absorbed five general objections to the doctrine of the Real Presence in my formative years as a Christian (summarized below). It should be noted that the first four objections attempt only to refute the doctrine without erecting anything in its place, whereas the fifth, resting on the validity of its predecessors, does attempt an alternative explanation of what Jesus instituted at the Last Supper. The objections are:

1. That God forbids human sacrifice, rendering impossible the Catholic understanding of the bread and wine as the literal Body and Blood of Jesus.

2. That the doctrine adds to the once-for-all sacrifice of Christ on Golgotha by sacrificing

Christ again in the "Sacrifice of the Mass."

3. That Christ could not have commanded His disciples to drink His Blood, since such a command would be a violation of God's Word under both the Old and New Covenants.[5]

4. That the doctrine makes the Eucharist a form of idolatry and salvation by works.

5. That its true meaning is merely symbolic, enabling us to look back to the Cross as the Passover looked forward to it — a kind of audio-visual aid.

Objections 1 and 2:
Some Mental Ping-Pong

I began with the contention that the center of the Sacrifice of the Mass cannot be the Body and Blood of Christ since Scripture plainly forbids human sacrifice. This single objection, so enormously obvious, had been enough to keep me from concerning myself with the Real Presence for years. Naturally enough then, I turned to it first. I need not bother with the Real Presence at all, I reasoned, if it cannot stand up to this difficulty.

Having thus steeled myself for what I assumed

---

[5]Genesis 9:4; Leviticus 17:10-12; Acts 15:20, 28-29 — among others.

would be my biggest challenge, I was surprised to see the weight of this objection evaporate before my eyes. For it suddenly dawned on me that whether they accept the Real Presence or not, *all* orthodox Christians believe Jesus Christ was both Lamb of God and Son of Man; that is, that He was a human sacrifice. If we base our objection to the Real presence on the proposition "God always forbids human sacrifice," we ironically find ourselves in opposition to the testimony of Scripture.[6] The fact is, God forbids precisely every human sacrifice but the Sacrifice He makes of Himself.

Fair enough, I thought, but even granting that Christ was a human sacrifice, the Epistle to the Hebrews nonetheless says that His Sacrifice was done *"once* for all."[7]   If this is so, isn't all this business about the "Sacrifice of the Mass" a needless addition to His finished work on Calvary?

This seemed unanswerable — as long as I had thought of Christ's sacrifice in merely earthly terms. But then I began to grasp two things: (1) the Eternity and (2) the Humanity of Christ.

Christ Eternal: We who live inside time view the life of Jesus of Nazareth as a point on the line of history. Indeed, we split history into B.C. and A.D., thinking

---

[6]1 Corinthians 15:3, among endless other citations. (Or if you are into highlighting, just dip your New Testament in yellow ink. It's quicker.)

[7]Hebrews 10:10.

God, like us, has a past dribbling irretrievably away, a tiny present and an unpossessed future. That is, we think He is stuck to the "time line." But is He? He certainly does not talk that way. He says He is I AM from "everlasting to everlasting," that He "makes known the end from the beginning," that He is "the same, yesterday, today, and forever."[8] He describes Himself as the "Alpha and Omega, the One Who is and Who was and Who is to come."[9] Terms like "eternal," "omniscient," and "omnipresent," while fun to apply to the Internal Revenue Service, are nonetheless more fittingly applied to Him. In fact, when carefully considered, the biblical evidence overwhelmingly points to the fact that God is not mired in time as we are, but that He *surrounds* time and enters it at His choosing. Thus I found I had been encamped with the ancient Arameans. They thought God was present only on the mountains;[10] I thought God was present only in the present.

The Arameans and I were wrong. God dwells every*when* as well as everywhere. All times are present to Him just as all places and things are. If Jesus were only a finite creature, trapped inside time like us, we could relegate His life to the lumber room of the past along with the bombing of Pearl Harbor, the signing of the

---

[8]Psalm 90:2; Isaiah 46:10; Hebrews 13:8.
[9]Revelation 1:8.
[10]1 Kings 20:28.

Magna Carta or the battle of Waterloo. But since he is the Incarnate Eternal Word, He stands with one foot in time and one foot out of it. The Scripture expresses this in a fascinating way: it describes Him as the "Lamb slain from the foundation of the world."[11] This means, in effect, that the life, death and resurrection Jesus experienced "once for all" are His from all eternity. His sacrifice on Golgotha happened once *in time*, but it is a fact of His changeless Being right now, always and everywhere, before, after and beyond all worlds.[12] Christ transcends time because He invented it.

Christ the Son of Man: The eternity of Jesus Christ is an immense fact, but as we grasp it we often lose our grip on another fact: His complete and glorified Humanity. We vaguely begin to regard Him as God and "sort of" Man. This is demonstrated most clearly by our need to *explain* His questions and His professions of ignorance. We shift a little in our seats when we read that Jesus asked "Who touched me?," or expressed astonishment at the centurion's faith, or flatly stated that He did not know when the world would end.[13] We say something like "He did that for our benefit, or to demonstrate His humility." Yet we never feel this impulse to tidy up any of the disciples' questions. Why? Because we know that *they* are human beings and human

---

[11]Revelation 13:8.
[12]Malachi 3:6.
[13]Luke 8:45; Matthew 8:10; Matthew 24:36.

beings ask questions. But it is very hard, once we have believed in Jesus' deity, to conquer the notion that He only seemed human.

To a certain extent this notion is quite natural; the mind boggles at the thought of cramming into a human body the Power that hurled the Andromeda Galaxy. But "natural" does not necessarily equal "true." Indeed, in the first century, difficulty with the concept of the Incarnation metastasized into one of the earliest errors in Christian history. This was Docetism, which held the Humanity of Christ to be a sort of holy illusion sent by God. It is precisely this misguided zeal for God's transcendence that is combated in 1 John 4:2: "This is how you can recognize God's Spirit: every spirit that acknowledges Jesus Christ come *in the flesh* belongs to God."

The false distinction between physical and spiritual is a danger nearly all biblical Christians have fought since. On one front we find a throng of cults and modernist theologies cheerfully dispensing with the historic Jesus of Nazareth in a welter of disembodied cosmic Christs. But more insidiously, even committed Christians often find within themselves the same mainspring of unbelief taking the form of a hazy but persistent notion that Christ for some reason dissolved back into "pure spirituality" after His death. As C. S. Lewis says:

> . . . in our heart of hearts, we tend to slur over the
> risen *Manhood* of Christ, to conceive Him, after
> death, simply returning into Deity, so that the
> Resurrection would be no more than the reversal
> or undoing of the Incarnation.[14]

Our belief in the Resurrection, robust as far as it
goes, can sometimes be adulterated by our distrust of the
Incarnation. We can come to feel that His glorified
Humanity was show without substance; a grand finale
special effect to wow doubting Thomases. The *reductio
ad absurdum* of this error was apparent in the words of a
man I once heard who held that Christ shed His
glorified body at the Ascension because "He was
through using it." To be sure, the speaker was an honest
and decent man. But his words bespoke a world-view
equally conditioned by Christ the Lord and Henry Ford;
the ultimate seal of approval for planned obsolescence.

Jesus eating fish and bread, Jesus being touched,
Jesus scarred — such a spectacular display dazzled the
disciples into faith, but faith in what? Well, among other
things, faith in "the redemption of our bodies."[15] They
knew that God has not undone what He did at
Bethlehem, that the Incarnation of the Word is as eternal
as the Word Himself. He did not zip on a "man suit";
He became (and remains) Man. This is the glowing core

---

[14]C. S. Lewis, *Miracles* (New York: MacMillan
Publishing, 1947), p. 147.
[15]Romans 8:23.

of the Christian hope that He will "transform our lowly bodies so that they will be like His glorious body."[16] It is why Paul writes (after the Ascension) that "in Him all the fullness of the Deity dwells *in bodily form*" and that "there is one mediator between God and men, the *Man* Christ Jesus."[17] God has willed that the glorified Humanity of Christ be inseparably knit to His Deity. To divide them is to saw Our Lord in two.

Participation — Not Re-Sacrifice: What then becomes of the concern over sacrificing Christ again? The meaning of the eternal Humanity of Christ is something all Evangelicals live by every day: the fact that Jesus of Nazareth, a man born in Judea circa 4 B.C., is personally accessible to us here and now by simple faith. The Catholic Church also rejoices in this mystery, but in an even deeper way. Knowing that union with the God-Man Jesus necessarily means full union with His glorified Humanity, it has always believed that He provided the permanent means to share in that eternal reality when He offered the loaf and cup to His disciples with the words, "This is my Body. This is my Blood." The Church therefore speaks of the Eucharist as re-presenting, not re-sacrificing, Jesus Christ:

> The re-presentation means that on the cross, Jesus offered Himself and all His sufferings to God by

---

[16]Philippians 3:21.
[17]Colossians 2:9; 1 Timothy 2:5.

an immolation of Himself that brought on His physical death . . . On the altar, by reason of the glorified state of His human nature, "death has no more power over him" (Romans 6:9). *Consequently, the shedding of His Blood is impossible.*[18] Nevertheless, according to the plan of divine providence, the continued sacrifice of Christ is manifested . . . by the transubstantiation of bread into the Body of Christ and of wine into His Blood.[19]

This is a far cry from sacrificing Christ again. The key idea here is not repetition of His death (which the Church plainly states is impossible), but our present *participation* in the one eternal sacrifice of Christ on Calvary. We drink each day from the well He dug once for all; we eat the one loaf He has prepared. This language, used since the very beginning of the church,[20] was affirmed at the Council of Trent and re-affirmed at Vatican II:

The benefits of this oblation (the bloody one, that is) are received in abundance through this unbloody oblation. By no means, then, does the

---

[18]Italics mine.

[19]John A. Hardon, S. J., *The Catholic Catechism* (Garden City, NY: Doubleday & Co., Inc., 1975), p. 466.

[20]"Is not the cup of thanksgiving for which we give thanks a participation in the blood of Christ? And is not the bread we break a participation in the body of Christ?" (1 Corinthians 10:16).

sacrifice of the Mass detract from the sacrifice of the cross.[21]

Therefore, I concluded, my fears on this score were unfounded. The sacrifice of the Mass does not add to the sacrifice of the Cross any more than prayers for our daily bread add to God's providence. Rather, as the offering of our prayers is *part* of God's providence and not a useless addition to it, so the sacrifice of the Mass is incorporated into the Cross. The Real Presence, if it is true, is the place we denizens of time can taste most fully the eternity of Christ crucified and risen. If the Catholic Eucharist is His Body and Blood, it is because it depends on, and in no way supersedes, the Cross.

Objections 3 and 4:
A Herring Snack
and a Wrestling Match

When I arrived at the third objection I put away my mental ping-pong paddle. The contention that the Real Presence contradicts scriptural injunctions against eating blood has always struck me as futile. To my mind, few things were more obvious than that Jesus, in Mark 7:17-

---

[21]Council of Trent, *The Doctrine on the Most Holy Sacrifice of the Mass*, II: Denzinger 940 (1743).

19, removed all Old Testament dietary restrictions. This left the Council of Jerusalem's letter to Gentile Christians[22] as the sole place in the New Testament where I could find the barest thread of a law against eating blood. Yet it seems clear to me that the purpose of this injunction was not to override Christ's declaration, but to prevent wounding the conscience of the Jewish community (see v. 21). The Council was actually performing an act of charity in response to a particular cultural setting, not laying down an eternal decree. This is borne out by the writings of one of the key figures in that Council, the Apostle Paul. He unhesitatingly states in 1 Corinthians 8 that food sacrificed to idols (another prohibited item according to the Jerusalem Council) is utterly harmless except for its power to defile the conscience of the weaker brother. And he reiterates this in Romans 14:14 with the words, "As one who is in the Lord Jesus, I am fully convinced that no food is unclean in itself."

All this, plus the fact that virtually no Christian I know would think twice about eating a juicy red sirloin, left me with no qualms. When the testimony of Christ, the witness of the Scriptures and the practice of the Church lined up in such a fashion, there was little to do but snack on this kosher red herring and find bigger fish to fry.

So it was that I arrived at the fourth objection, that

---

[22] Acts 15:19-29, 21:25.

the Eucharistic Real Presence is a form of idolatry and salvation by works. For me and many like me, this issue was an emotional as well as theological wrestling match. If anything cuts Evangelicals to the quick, it is the holy fear of idolatry and righteousness by works. With one voice the Evangelical battalion in the army of God shouts, "You shall have no gods before Him and you shall not set aside His grace. For if righteousness could be gained through the law, Christ died for nothing!"[23] Where I come from this is the rock-bottom gospel. Thus it is not difficult to imagine my visceral reaction to adoration of the Eucharist as the very Presence of Jesus. I wondered whether I was being tempted to worship the golden calf. Likewise, the idea of the sacrament as a "means of grace" was deeply disturbing. It looked exactly like a pagan mechanism for earning the approval of a hateful god. Nor was I alone in feeling this way. For such fears impel many devout Christians to shun belief in the Real Presence.

To my mind, this is very healthy. It shows a passionate concern about the abuses of the past and a burning love of the freedom that is in Christ. Still, we must not allow our fears to hinder our obedience to Paul's urging: "Test everything. Hold on to the good."[24] Otherwise, as Paul's teacher, Rabbi Gamaliel, warned and he himself discovered, it is not unthinkable

---

[23]Exodus 20:2; Galatians 2:21.
[24]1 Thessalonians 5:21.

that we should find ourselves wrestling the Everlasting Arm.

Focusing Our Fears: It is often harder than might be supposed to immediately voice all the gut feelings percolating at the bottom of Objection 4 in an orderly way. For such things reach right down through the trauma of a splintered Christendom to the very roots of monotheism. Any serious attempt to settle the question demands that we labor to disentangle it from a whole mass of irrelevancies and logical fallacies — a sticky task for us sinners. My own examination revealed that this objection was composed of a cluster of the following roots:

A. The feeling that "physical" and "spiritual" are somehow intrinsically opposed. Verses like "We walk by faith, not by sight"[25] appeared to lend weight to this sentiment.

B. The legitimate dread of idolatry. How can a Christian in good conscience possibly adore the Eucharist? Is it not plainly blasphemous? This sentiment was energized by passages such as "They exchanged the truth of God for a lie, and worshipped and served created things rather than the Creator."[26]

C. The stumbling block of locality. How can Christ, Who is everywhere, be any more present in the bread and wine?

---

[25]2 Corinthians 5:7 (KJV).
[26]Romans 1:25.

D. The mistrust of ritual — that is, of a repetitive physical act — as being somehow necessarily a "religion of works" — a way to earn brownie points. Paired with this were misgivings about calling the Eucharist a "means of grace": the outrageous proposition that God channels real life-changing power through the consecrated bread and wine.

Problems A and B — Sacrament or Idol?: It will be seen at once that the first of these four roots was partially exposed by my earlier discoveries. Christ's Risen Humanity had already shown me that the opposition of physical to spiritual was our idea, not His. It is fallout from the Fall, not intrinsic to the universe. For Adam, not Christ, fractured God's handiwork.

We wrecked Creation by making a grab and saying, "This much of it shall be our own." The fabric ripped. Now, instead of the sacred seamlessness in which every fiber of Creation was knit together in a pattern that blazoned the glory of God, we had a torn garment. The poor remnant we clutched in our fists was *secular*, in the most tragic sense of the word: that which is not acknowledged as God's.[27]

Emotionally, at least, I had tended to equate

---

[27]Thomas Howard, *Evangelical Is Not Enough* (San Francisco: Ignatius Press, 1984), p. 30.

"physical" — the riot of gravity, kangaroos, bureaucrats, birthday candles, auto mechanics, brontosaurus skeletons, and quasars — with "secular," that which is not acknowledged as God's.   Of course, in some amorphous sense, I had held that "the earth is the Lord's."   But my day-to-day life had for years reduced such statements to mere mental diagrams.   In practice I regarded prayer as somehow more spiritual than sitting on a committee, preaching as more anointed than plumbing.   Only the revelation of Christ's Humanity infused vigor into my bloodless theoretical doctrine. Through Him, my eyes were opened to the biblical teaching that the Incarnation and our participation in it restores Creation.   As Paul says:

> The creation waits in eager expectation for the sons of God to be revealed. For the creation was subjected to frustration, not by its own choice, but by the will of the one who subjected it, in hope that the creation itself will be liberated from its bondage to decay and brought into the glorious freedom of the children of God.[28]

And Thomas Howard writes:

> The Incarnation, then, transfigures the whole fabric of life for us and delivers it back to us and us back to it in the seamlessness that we lost at our exile from Eden. Once again we may stand in our

---

[28]Romans 8:19-21.

proper relation to things, as lords over them and not as their slaves. Once more we stand in our true Adam-like dignity because of the Second Adam and may begin to learn anew the solemn office for which we were created, namely, to bless God and to lead the whole Creation in that blessing. Our flesh, having been worn by the Most High Himself is the most noble mantle of all. The Manichaeans and Buddhists and Platonists on the one hand, who belittle this flesh, and the gluttons and lechers and egoists on the other, who are slaves to it, are still living in division. Only in the Incarnation may we find the knitting back together of the fabric into its true integrity.[29]

The Word made flesh, then, is the sign that this torn world is being mended, not split into a sheer dichotomy. "Physical" and "spiritual" will cease their quarreling at the Lamb's Wedding Feast; they will be Bride and Groom through the Risen Body of Christ.

In fact, the Incarnation is the only means of reconciling them and the sole doorway into a right understanding of their relationship. Here and here alone is the Creation renewed, neither melted in a New Age pantheistic soup nor denied as essentially secular.

Seeing this, I experienced a kind of déjà vu. As with the issue of human sacrifice, it dawned on me that *no* orthodox Christian, Protestant or Catholic, worships

---

[29]Howard, *Evangelical Is Not Enough*, p. 33.

the Deity of Jesus apart from His created Humanity. To do so is, as we have seen from 1 John 4:2, unbiblical. No Christian rebukes Thomas' cry, "My Lord and My God!," though his words were spoken to a Man.[30] Nor do we exalt a mere Ground of Being or Christ Consciousness. We worship an older Brother whose hands know the feel of cedar, whose feet know the dust of the hills, and whose heart was pierced with a Roman lance. Here, at least, we Evangelicals *do* find ourselves at home with the sacramental principle. Here, at least, Protestants and Catholics unite around one of the great paradoxes of the gospel: No man may be worshipped; yet the Son of Man must be adored.

This paradox is absolutely central to dealing with the issue of supposed idolatry of the Blessed Sacrament. It confronted me with the fact that since God can unite with His Creation in the human body of Jesus, there is no reason He cannot do so in the Eucharist. If God visits us in the bread and wine as he has in the flesh of Christ, then worship of the Eucharist is no more sinful than Thomas' prostration before the Risen One. The charge of idolatry, therefore, begged the question by assuming I knew the Real Presence to be false when, in fact, I did not. And this was the crux of the matter. If I found the Real Presence to be untrue, then worship of the Eucharist is indeed idolatrous. But if the Eucharist *is* the actual Body and Blood of the Lord, then visceral

---

[30]John 20:24-28.

reaction or no, the adoration accorded it is holy and pleasing to God.

Problems C and D — Narrow "Religion" or Divine Encounter?: Problem C, what I call the stumbling block of locality, is simply this: Is it not foolish to confine the omnipresent Christ to physical objects? How can He Who fills all in all possibly be narrowed to a bit of bread and a sip of wine? The whole thing bristles with hazard and absurdity. My Protestant blood, nurtured as it had been on tales of Tetzel's indulgences and the legalistic abominations of the late medieval ages, dreads the thought of our transcendent God becoming the prisoner of ecclesiastical tyrants — cooped up like a false Aslan in a stable.[31] Viewed from this perspective, the Real Presence seemed both intolerably risky and arrogant. Why would God send His free gift of grace through such narrow channels; things which can be withheld from the faithful by wicked men? And what of non-Eucharistic Christians? Does the Real Presence imply that they are not "really" experiencing God?

This is quite an onslaught. But though the questions are many I think it fairly plain they radiate from one central issue: the fear of man's monopolizing access to God. And to be sure, this is a legitimate fear. It is no secret that some excommunications and

---

[31]If my meaning here is obscure, grab a copy of C. S. Lewis' *The Last Battle* some rainy Saturday afternoon and give yourself a treat!

interdicts[32] were tainted with pretty sleazy motives. Nor does it stop there. Our entire history, littered as it is with Stalinist power grabs, cheesy charlatans and all manner of jiggery-pokery, testifies that we are infected with the hellish desire to own the Godhead. That is what the Fall is.

Yet for all that, our fallenness has nothing to do with whether the Real Presence is true. The mere fact that a thing is capable of corrupt use by our soiled hands says nothing about the essence of that thing. Otherwise, the very Gospel itself, committed as it has been into our care, would be worthless. The argument from risk is thus no argument at all. It is simply another way of saying that free will is a knotty problem and God ought to be more cautious the next time He makes a universe.

Further, it is a mistake to assume that the Catholic Church calls the Eucharist the sole avenue of Christ's Presence among His people. Pope Paul VI, in his encyclical *Mysterium Fidei*, identified no less than eight ways in which Christ is present to believers apart from the Eucharist (e.g. through Scripture, prayer, acts of charity, the Holy Spirit in fellow believers, etc.) He states:

---

[32]An interdict could forbid a person, a district, a city or a whole nation from receiving all sacraments (including the Eucharist and Christian burial). Originally intended to stem the tide of certain forms of individual and corporate sin, the power of interdict was used now and then by corrupt popes to pressure secular rulers into towing the line.

> This presence is called *real* — by which it is not intended to exclude all other types of presence as if they could not be 'real' too, but because it is presence in the fullest sense. It is a substantial presence by which Christ, the God-man, is wholly and entirely present.[33]

Thus I saw that, so far from implying the exclusion of all other forms of Christian spirituality, the Real Presence instead ratifies them. That is because, according to the Church, the Eucharist is centered in the very heart of Christianity — in the Incarnation, Death and Resurrection of Jesus. As the Gospel consummates rather than cancels the Law, so the Real Presence consummates all the various ways in which we touch our Lord. To stumble over locality as a violation of God's omnipresence is, therefore, to miss the point of His becoming human in Christ. Certainly He is always with us. Certainly non-Eucharistic Christians have a valid relationship with Him. That is precisely the point. For the Eucharist, if the Real Presence is true, is the most concentrated manifestation of what they experience every day. Both Scripture and experience testify that our hearts thirst to be *met* by God. We long to say with Jacob, "Surely the LORD is in this place!"[34] But our souls cannot feed on mere abstract omnipresence; we

---

[33]Paul VI, *Mysterium Fidei*, IV, 35-39.
[34]Genesis 28:16.

hunger for a *touch*. In the Eucharist, says the Church, God touches us. We meet Him there most fully.

As John A. Hardon, S. J. writes:

> If we could make a graphic comparison, there is as much difference between Christ's presence in the Blessed Sacrament and His presence elsewhere on earth as there was between His presence among the disciples when He appeared to them on Easter Sunday night and His presence in their midst before and after the appearance.[35]

This realization knocked my stumbling block off the path entirely. I saw that the idea of locality, uncomfortable as it may be, was nevertheless scriptural. If it is a risk, it is a risk God took when His only begotten Son became flesh and dwelt among us. Defying our insistence on caution, He indeed allowed Himself to be cooped up in a stable — in Bethlehem. That is why He is a Stone that makes men stumble; it is also why He is the source of our hope. The Incarnation is not God's prison — it is our liberation. For as C. S. Lewis says, "The world which would not know Him as present everywhere was saved by His becoming *local*."[36]

In Christ, the broad daylight of God is focused to a pinpoint that a world might be kindled. If, therefore, the same thing happens through the lens of the

---

[35]Hardon, *The Catholic Catechism*, p. 465.
[36]Lewis, *Miracles*, p. 140.

Eucharist, we cannot balk that this is foreign to the Scriptures.

By now I was feeling a tad masochistic — wrestled as I was into a near hammerlock, yet still doggedly issuing challenges. My one remaining trump card was my suspicion that Eucharistic ritual and "dead religion" were somehow synonymous. But why this was so I found hard to define at first. Because ritual is physical? By now I was quite certain that mere physicality had no bearing on whether a thing is of God. Because it is repetitive? The Lord's Prayer has been ceaselessly repeated for two millenia, yet no Christian would thus discard *it* as a dead work. I therefore had to ask myself why, precisely, ritual troubled me if its two essential elements, physicality and repetitiveness, are kosher. That question led me to the real heart of the problem: my suspicion of the idea, implicit in the doctrine of the Real Presence, that the Eucharist is a "means of grace."

Quite simply, this notion seemed to run counter to most of what I understood of God's free gift. In the tradition that nurtured me, God is the One Who breaks our religious chains and shatters punctilious legalism. We do not have to jump through hoops and prove our worthiness to get Him to love us. It is He, not we, who makes all the overtures. My Christianity was formed around the liberating truth that God's grace is accessible here and now by simple faith in Jesus. We do not have to earn it; we have only to accept it. This is, of course, a fact deeply rooted in Scripture. "It is by grace you have been saved, through faith," said Paul, "And this not from yourselves, it is the gift of God — not by works, so that no one can boast."[37] No red tape, no rigamarole, no "good deeds" required.

Why then, I wondered, was this deed different? If there is anything a good Protestant suspects, it is an intermediary between us and the grace of Christ. Such a thing seems contrary to the very idea of boldly approaching the Throne. It carries the aroma of bureaucracy, waiting lines and paperwork. Simple, believing prayer ought to be "means of grace" enough, I thought. Anything else — and particularly any ritual — seemed to constitute earning salvation and rejecting the finished work of Christ.

This difficulty is, of course, a classic one. It is often used as an illustration of how Christians can lose the simplicity of the Gospel and become enmeshed in a false spirit of circumcision like the Galatians. In the Protestantism of my roots the notion of the Eucharist (or, for that matter, anything else) as a means of grace looked exactly like the sort of human tradition condemned by Christ.[38] Its origin, we were certain, lay in a neglect of the Word of God which had allowed "religion" to creep in like fossilizing sediment and change the living faith to stone. Naturally then, the only

---

[37]Ephesians 2:8-9.
[38]Texts like Mark 7:6-13 seemed to support this.

solution to the problem was a return to our foundations and a renewing work of the Spirit by the Scriptures. To reverse the situation we must, it was said, let go of "the traditions of the elders" and hold fast to the commands of God.

So hold fast I did. And indeed the Scriptures proved to be, in many ways, precisely the tonic I had hoped. In their light I saw not only my sin but God's atoning grace. Through them I tasted Christ and experienced His revelation. By continually steeping my mind in their truth I found myself progressively set free by the Spirit to love God more fully. And not only I, but millions of Christians know the same reality. Here, I thought, was proof that the Living God is encountered by faith alone. Such simplicity seemed to dispel the need for any "means of grace . . ." Until, ironically, I recalled my pastor's exegesis of the Bread of Life discourse in John 6.

Do not misunderstand. My pastor was certainly was no exponent of Catholic theology. Rather, in classic Evangelical fashion, this good man held that "the teaching of Christ is the true bread from heaven" and that the passage had no Eucharistic significance. He then reminded us that a Kingdom populated by milk-fed "fat babies" is not the goal of Our Lord's command to be like children. We must not imagine, he would say, that unenlightened "Me and Jesus" Christianity bore any resemblance to the apostolic preaching. Instead, he urged, we must mature in Christ by "eating His word" and relying on the grace of God working in and through fellow Bible-believing Christians. Only thus, said he, could we hope to grow.

Now none of this was, in itself, shocking or new. But juxtaposed with my doubts about means of grace, the effect was dramatic. It suddenly bore in on me that this grasp of biblical teaching as "food for maturity" was strikingly similar to the Catholic understanding of the Eucharist. I saw at once that regular biblical fellowship and regular Holy Communion were both a form of ritual; both "means of grace." The only difference is that in the former, God transubstantiates paper, ink and the human voice into His Word; whereas in the latter, according to Catholics, He changes the bread and wine into something even more impressive. My difficulty, then, was not with the idea of ritual "means of grace" as such, but with a God Who might touch me in a non-verbal, non-cerebral, non-"spiritual" way.

This dawning awareness threw new light on my thoughts. Looking again into Scripture I began to see a God Who, so far from shunning any means of grace, instead nearly always manifests Himself through what He has made. Moreover, the Bible emphatically denied the demand that this manifestation be strictly verbal. Psalm 19, for example, testifies to the loud praise given God by the silent, wheeling heavens. And Paul agrees to this, declaring the primal form of God's revelation to be the wordless, brute fact of the Creation itself.[39] Again and again throughout the Bible we see God working in and through, not only words, but tempests, hands, armies, shepherd's staffs, whirlwinds, muddy rivers — even skeletal remains![40] And all this is capped by the scandal of the Incarnation: Jesus Christ — the ultimate means of grace.

At this point it may be asked whether I am indulging in a vague pantheism and denying Jesus His place as sole Mediator of the New Covenant. Not at all. Paul, in 1 Timothy 2:5, clearly says He is. But this does not stop the Apostle from speaking of his own "administration of God's grace."[41] Nor does it stifle his declaration that the manifold wisdom of God will be made known through the church.[42] Still less does it keep Christ's power from flowing, not only through believers, but even through inanimate objects such as clothes and handkerchiefs.[43] Thus we may, in Paul's phrase, describe all Creation as an earthen vessel intended to show forth the glory of God by its very earthiness.[44] God and His

---

[39]Romans 1:20.

[40]That's right. Skeletal remains. See 2 Kings 13:21 for the peculiar incident to which I refer.

[41]Ephesians 3:2.

[42]Ephesians 3:10.

[43]See Luke 5:27-28 and Acts 19:11-12. Also note the fascinating hint of Mark 9:2-3; not just Christ's body, but his very clothes are transfigured and share in His glory.

[44]2 Corinthians 4:7.

redeemed Creation are neither identical nor enemies, but complementary. For this reason, Scripture neither blurs the distinction between God and Nature nor pits Christ's mediatorship against any means of grace He may use. The Sovereign Lord is utterly free to meet us either verbally, as in prayer and Scripture, or non-verbally, in the consecrated bread and wine. For He is, after all, the Word made flesh, not merely the Word made word.

Seeing this, I knew that Objection 4 had shot its bolt. Three of the four pegs on which it hung were already yanked from the wall; now the fourth was gone as well. For I had charged that ritual "means of grace" equalled "works religion." But I had instead found that God manifests Himself via many means of grace, including ritual. And I still had no solid basis to claim that Christ did not mean exactly what He said when He told the Apostles, "This is My Body. This is My Blood."[45]

Therefore, I concluded, to call the Real Presence a form of salvation by works was to again beg the question. Since I had no shred of evidence that Christ's words should be taken at something other than face value, I could not declare the Eucharist a false means of grace. If it *is* the Body and Blood of Christ (which I had not refuted), then it is par excellence a channel of blessing through which God comes to us — a means of grace. And to receive grace in any form is to reject, not

---

[45]Matthew 26:26-28; 1 Corinthians 10:16, 11:23-27.

sanctify, the vanity of earned salvation. Thus rather than burying a dead work I was forced to concede the living truth of this Catholic teaching. For when Objection 4 collapsed, so did my entire case against the Real Presence.

Objection 5:
Judo-Christian Theology

His entire case?, you ask. But what of Objection 5? Did I not say that the Eucharist is merely symbolic and intended simply as an aid to memory? Surely this has not been disproved. Why give up the fight now?

Because the fifth objection rests its credentials entirely on the validity of the other four. Had I found in them reason to discredit the Real Presence, I could have proposed the memorial aspect of the Eucharist as an "alternative explanation." But since I could not find any such reason, the need for an alternative vanished.

This does not mean however that Objection 5 disappeared altogether. For the full Catholic understanding of the Eucharist has never in the least denied the words, "Do this in remembrance of Me."[46] It has only taken issue with the claim that symbolism and mere memorial dispel the mystery of the Real Presence.

---

[46] 1 Corinthians 11:24-25.

The Greek word "anamnesis" like its English counterpart "remembrance" means not only "to recall," but "to make present." For, of course, we remember not only past events but present facts. (As when I remember, for example, both my tenth birthday and the fact that I must return books to the library today. The latter is no recall of the past, but a focus on present reality.) In a similar vein, our Lord's command to remember enhances, not contradicts, the Real Presence. For as we have seen, though the events of the Passion are past; the reality of the Passion is eternally intended for our participation. In the words of John A. Hardon, S. J.:

> When we say that the Mass commemorates Christ's death, we mean that in a mysterious way Christ really offers Himself as the eternal priest and that His oblation is not only a psychological remembrance but a mystical reality. When we say that the Mass is a memorial of His Resurrection, this too is not merely a mental recollection. After all, the Christ Who is now in heaven and the principal priest at the altar is the risen Savior. His Resurrection is not only an event that took place once, but a continuing fact of salvation history. To call the Mass a memorial of the Resurrection may conjure up the image of a pleasant memory that swiftly crosses the mind. It should rather tell us that in the Mass the risen Lord is present and in our midst and bids us unite ourselves, still mortal, with Him Who is our Resurrection."[47]

---

[47]Hardon, *The Catholic Catechism*, p. 467.

Thus, in a kind of Judo move, the very strength of my argument was turned against itself. Objection 5, rather than being flatly disproved, was instead welcomed back to its place as a *part* of ancient Catholic teaching.

A Fresh Look at the Real Presence

So my theological house, once littered with reasons to disbelieve in the Real Presence, was now spic 'n span. What was more, my hard look at Scripture had not just undermined my objections, but made the Catholic case very attractive indeed. For the piercing beauty of this ancient teaching not only made sense, it aroused a spiritual hunger. I could not dispassionately cock my eyebrow as if I had merely discovered a curious knick-knack in the attic; I was being approached by the living God and I knew it. Moreover, I was well aware of our Lord's warning that a house swept clean and empty is a standing invitation to a demonic beer bust. Therefore, I resolved to reoccupy mine through a fresh look at the Real Presence. I now knew that the doctrine was not *un*biblical; what was the evidence in its favor?

Well, for starters, the plain sense of Christ's own words. For Jesus nowhere hints that He speaks in a parable when He says to the crowd at Capernaum, "I am the living bread that came down from heaven. If a man eats of this bread he will live forever. This bread is my flesh, which I will give for the life of the world."[48]

His hearers, at least, took His words as something other than symbolic. "How can this man give us his flesh to eat?" they kvetched. Yet as He would do before Caiaphas, Jesus made no attempt to soften His language. Instead He drove the point home with the words, "I tell you the truth, unless you eat the flesh of the Son of Man and drink his blood, you have no life in you." Why? Because, as He says, His flesh is real food, His blood is real drink, and whoever partakes remains in Him, and He in them. This ought to sound familiar. For it is precisely the same language of *participation* we discussed earlier — a participation not only in His Spirit, but in His Humanity as well.

Not that this was appreciated by His hearers, of course. Yet neither was it utterly misunderstood. In fact, a great crowd of shocked disciples (who knew only too well what He meant) abandoned Him then and there. Yet even this crisis did not move Jesus to "explain what He was really driving at."

So what?, you may ask. Jesus alienated a lot of people without apology. And indeed some do see in this passage nothing more than a test of faith: crazy-like-a-fox Jesus baffling His shallow hangers-on with outrageous parables. But it does not wash. For Mark

---

[48]John 6:51. But read the whole chapter to get your bearings.

tells us that Jesus *always* explained His peculiar figures of speech to His befuddled Apostles.[49] Yet on this occasion, He turns to the Twelve and says only "Well? Are you leaving too?" and nothing else. No word of explanation. No deeper inner meaning. Nothing. In fact, the whole exchange is strikingly similar to His thrice-stated prophecies of impending death and Resurrection. In both cases His disciples were baffled, squinting to read between the lines and discussing among themselves what He might *really* mean. And in both cases He did not "clarify" Himself — evidently because, in both cases, He was stating a bald fact.[50]

Moreover, He compounded this by indulging in identical language with these same disciples at the Last Supper. Identifying Himself with the Passover (and again without "clarification"), He took the loaf and cup and declared them to be His Body and Blood. Period. In other words, He gave the Twelve no point of reference apart from the memory of His puzzling discourse at Capernaum and the mystifying prophecy of His death and Resurrection. What they made of all this at the time is, of course, anyone's guess. Most likely their grasp was almost nil. What matters is that He promised them further light — a light shed by the Holy Spirit and the events of the next three days.[51] When that

---

[49]Mark 4:34.
[50]Mark 8:31-32, 9:9-10.
[51]John 16:12-16.

light dawned on Easter morning the Apostles saw just how baldly factual Christ could be. Why then should we be surprised if they also took literally His word about the bread and wine? Indeed, if Jesus meant to be understood symbolically, He could not have chosen a more misleading approach.

Nor do we have a particle of evidence that the Apostles did so understand Him. On the contrary, every shred of New Testament evidence points to an apostolic faith in the Real Presence from day one. Note, for example, that Paul, in his account of the Eucharist, explicitly states he is "delivering" what he "received" from the Lord.[52] "Receiving" and "delivering" are technical rabbinic terms meaning "to pass on a teaching in its entirety." In other words, Paul is saying that he teaches what the Twelve teach. Note further the likeness of Paul's account of the Last Supper to that of the first three Gospels (writings which are separated by considerable time and distance).[53] Their striking similarity to one another demonstrates that the Eucharistic story was set in liturgical concrete by the Church very rapidly after the events of the Passion — in other words, by the Twelve. Thus both the Gospels and Paul's own lips proclaim that his teaching about the Eucharist echoes that of Peter, James, John and the gang.

---

[52] 1 Corinthians 11:23.
[53] 1 Corinthians 11:23-25; Matthew 26:26-28; Mark 14:22-24; Luke 22:19-20.

And what is that teaching? Well, it looks for all the world like the Catholic understanding of the words, "This is My Body. This is My Blood." Paul, like the Gospels, quotes these words without qualification. Moreover, as we have already seen, he calls the Eucharist a "participation" in the Body and Blood of Christ.[54] But most startlingly, he declares that "whoever eats the bread or drinks the cup in an unworthy manner will be guilty of sinning against the Body and Blood of the Lord."[55] This verse has often been the focus of Herculean efforts to "explain its true meaning." Typically, it is torqued into a mere reference to sinning against fellow Christians. But this is vanity. For nowhere else in Scripture or subsequent Christian writings do we find the Church called the "Body and Blood of the Lord"; the phrase *always* refers to the Eucharist.

Nor is that all. For if the Real Presence is authentic apostolic teaching, we should expect to find a growing body of witnesses to it among those whom the Apostles taught. And we do. Indeed it is not too much to call the postbiblical record a massive and ever-swelling testimony to the early church's faith in the Real Presence.

Ignatius of Antioch, for example, in his epistle to the Smyrnaeans (c. 100), noted that belief in the Real Presence was one of the litmus tests of orthodoxy. He

---

[54] 1 Corinthians 10:16.
[55] 1 Corinthians 11:23.

spoke of "those who hold strange doctrines. . . . They abstain from Eucharist and prayer, because they allow not that the Eucharist is the flesh of our Saviour Jesus Christ." Similarly, Justin Martyr (c. 152) emphasized its apostolic origins, saying *"we have been taught* that the food which has been eucharized by the word of prayer from Him is the flesh and blood of the Incarnate Jesus."[56] And Irenaeus (who was a disciple of Polycarp, himself a disciple of the Apostle John) wrote circa 185, ". . . the bread, which is produced from the earth, when it receives the invocation of God, is no longer common bread, but the Eucharist, consisting of two realities, earthly and heavenly."[57]

Further, Athanasius (c. 296-323), who almost single-handedly withstood the Arian heresy, said, "When the great and wondrous prayers have been recited, then the bread becomes the Body and the cup the Blood of our Lord Jesus Christ."[58] And to this growing chorus of voices down the centuries were added Basil, Gregory of Nyssa, Hilary, Ambrose, Augustine, Chrysostom, Thomas Aquinas, Francis of Assisi, Clare, Teresa of Avila, John of the Cross, John Henry Newman, G. K. Chesterton, Flannery O'Connor, Padre Pio, Mother Teresa and innumerable hosts of others, living and dead.

In fact, even the Great Reformers acknowledged

---

[56]Justin Martyr, First Apology, 66, 2.
[57]Irenaeus, Contra Haereticos, 4, 18, 5.
[58]Athanasius, Sermon to the Baptized.

the profound mystery of the Eucharist. This is not, of course, to say that they espoused the complete Catholic doctrine on this point; many quite obviously did not. But the vast majority of them are still far closer to Rome than to Evangelicalism in their understanding of the Real Presence.

John Calvin, for example, though certainly no friend of Rome sounds remarkably Roman when he writes in his *Short Treatise on the Holy Supper*:

> It is a spiritual mystery which cannot be seen by the eye nor comprehended by human understanding. Therefore it is represented for us by means of visible signs, according to the need of our weakness. Nevertheless it is not a naked figure, but one joined to its truth and substance. With good reason then, the bread is called Body, because it not only represents, but also presents it.

Similarly, John Wycliffe said that the Eucharistic prayer of consecration "effects the presence of the Body of Christ. . . . Not that the bread is destroyed, but that it signifies the Body of the Lord there present in the sacrament."[59] Likewise, John Hus wrote, "The humble priest doth not . . . say that he is the creator of Christ, but that the Lord Christ by His power and word, through him, causes that which is bread to be His Body; not that at that time it began to be His, but that there on

---

[59]John Wycliffe, De Eucharistia, 100f.

the altar begins to be sacramentally in the form of the bread what previously was not there and therein." Martin Luther also believed this, writing in his *Small Catechism*, "What is the Sacrament of the Altar? It is the true Body and Blood of Christ under the bread and wine."

In short, there was not so much a flow of evidence for the Real Presence as an avalanche. Not only was I out of arguments against it, but the cascade of testimony *for* it from ancient, modern, Catholic and Protestant authorities was well-nigh overwhelming. What else could I do but believe?

The Plot Thickens

So it looked as if my journey was nearly over and my final step an obvious and easy one. I was now certain that the Real Presence was true. What was more, I now knew that because of it the Eucharist was not optional since its implications are ultimately as extreme as those of the deity of Christ. Both confront us with God incarnate. Both are either insanity, lies or truth. And both demand nothing less than worship and active faith, not mere mental assent. For it is in Jesus Christ, Who is fully present in the Eucharist, that all other means of grace (such as teaching and preaching) find their focus. Therefore, I saw that it was absolutely essential I respond not merely by believing in the Real Presence but by doing something about it. It was not enough that I just hear the word and so deceive myself — I had to "take and eat" even as I was commanded.

"Very well," I thought, "Next time I go to church I will do just that and believe with all my heart in the Real Presence!" But this intention suddenly raised a crucial point: namely, that *the Real Presence lies not in our subjective attitude to the Eucharist, but in an objective, Spirit-wrought change of the bread and wine into the actual Body and Blood of Christ.*

Like the Resurrection, the Real Presence matters only insofar as it is a thing "out there" and not a mere psychological projection originating in the mind of the believer. In other words, the Eucharist is either changed or it is not, just as Christ is either risen or He is not. And if the Eucharistic change is a fact, then it is a fact not just in our hearts but even for those who disbelieve it. Similarly, if the Eucharist is *not* the Body and Blood, then no amount of self-willed "faith" on my part could make it otherwise. Thus, much as I would have liked to, I realized I could not rush off to my local Evangelical church and "consecrate in my heart" the unconsecrated bread and grape juice I received there any more than I could privately write my own Scriptures or declare myself an Apostle.

For the change in the bread and wine can only be accomplished by the authority and power of the Lord

Christ Himself.   And this authority, according to
Scripture and Catholic teaching, has been delegated by
Christ to the Church solely through His Apostles.   As
Justin Martyr writes:

> The Apostles in their memoirs, which are called
> Gospels, have handed down what Jesus ordered
> *them* to do; that He took bread and, after giving
> thanks, said: "Do this in remembrance of me; this
> is My Body."   In like manner He took also the
> chalice, gave thanks, and said, "This is My Blood."
> *And to them only did He give it.*[60]

This hung me on the horns of a dilemma. I had to ask
where, logically, this apostolic authority to consecrate
the Eucharist now resides since the Apostles are no
longer with us.   In the majority opinion of a given
congregation? Quite simply, there is not the slightest bit
of support for this notion from Scripture or historic
Christianity. In the priesthood of all believers? As Justin
Martyr noted, the Gospels nowhere say that the power
to consecrate the Eucharist was delegated to all believers
indiscriminately. On the contrary, only to the Apostles
did Jesus say "Do this" on the night He was betrayed.[61]
And these Apostles themselves bestowed their Christ-
given authority, not on all their converts, but only on
certain men among them (e.g. Timothy and Titus) to act

---

[60]Justin Martyr, *First Apology*, 66 (Italics mine).
[61]Matthew 26:20-28, Mark 14:17-25, Luke 22:14-20.

as their successors and representatives on behalf of the whole Church. Finally, these successors were in turn commissioned to pass on their authority, not to everyone, but only to select individuals.[62]

The upshot of all this, according to Catholic teaching from ancient to modern times, is that it is only on these duly ordained successors — the bishops and priests of the apostolic Churches (e.g. Orthodox, Roman Catholic, Coptic, etc.) — that the Christ-bestowed power to consecrate the Eucharist rests.[63]

This was not, of course, to imply that the Catholic faith denies the believer's priesthood. It was simply to say, with Paul, that different members of the Body of Christ have different gifts and offices — "it was He Who gave some to be Apostles."[64] Nor was it to imply that Evangelical worship (or for that matter, any other form of Christian worship) is somehow illegitimate. God forbid! However, it was to acknowledge the fact that to seriously pursue the Real Presence inevitably meant a serious investigation of what Catholic theology calls "apostolic succession." And this issue of apostolic authority, in turn, raised an even deeper question, namely: If Jesus gave the office of Apostle only to a few Christians, and they in turn ordained not every believer but only certain chosen ones, precisely what grounds did

---

[62]Titus 1:5, 15.

[63]Second Vatican Council, *Decree on Ecumenism*, III, 14.

[64]Ephesians 4:11-13; 1 Corinthians 12:27-29.

I have for assuming an absolute egalitarianism among the Apostles themselves? The answer: none whatsoever.

Simon Peter: The Chief Apostle?

That meant the door was suddenly wide open to a claim I had never considered seriously before in my life: the Roman Catholic claim that apostolic authority and all that flows from it (including the Eucharist) was intended by Christ to find its center of gravity in the office of Peter, the "Chief Apostle."

This was an unsettling thought for my Evangelical stomach. I had been told quite early on in my Christian walk that, since God was no respecter of persons, all the Catholic claims for Peter as the "Chief Apostle" were utterly unbiblical. Yet now, as I examined the New Testament in light of what I had just learned, I suddenly found the evidence in favor of his primacy to be quite formidable: Simon Peter heads every list of Apostles given in the Gospels, he is typically portrayed as their spokesman, he alone is commissioned by Christ to strengthen his brothers and sisters when the Passion is over, he alone is thrice commanded to feed Christ's sheep, he alone received the Keys to the Kingdom at Caesarea Phillipi.[65] But most importantly, it is upon this

---

[65]Matthew 10:2-4, 16:13-16, 19; Luke 22:32; John

same Simon, whom Jesus surnamed Rock, that our Lord plainly pledged to build His Church.[66]

Of course, the question comes to mind: Why him? And the only answer seems to be "Because Christ chose him." At any rate, Peter certainly did not deserve it. Nor did he seem to have the foggiest notion of what Christ was up to when He commissioned him. (The very fact that he earned the appellation "Satan" from Christ minutes after He had received the Keys should attest to that!)[67] Yet all this only serves to buttress the Catholic claims about the primacy of his office by reinforcing the fact that it depends for its existence, not on the person of Peter, but on the grace of Jesus Christ. Further, since that office does not depend on the person of Peter, it is perfectly reasonable to assert that it was capable of continuing after his death. And this assertion becomes all the more certain, given the fact that Peter's office was established, not for his own glory, but as the Church's foundation.

> [The primacy of Peter] is considered legitimate because Jesus plainly intends to provide for his Church's future by establishing a regime that will not collapse with Peter's death.[68]

21:15-17.
    [66]Matthew 16:17-19.
    [67]Matthew 16:23.
    [68]*The Jerusalem Bible*, Notes on Matthew 16:19.

It follows, then, that if the Church is permanent, so also is the Rock upon which it is built — the bishop to whom Peter bequeathed his office before he was martyred: the bishop of Rome. And if that office is, by Christ's command, chief among those inheriting apostolic authority, then full union with Christ in the Eucharist logically demanded my full communion with the one to whom He gave that office.

So What Next?: Suggestions for Charting a Course

As I made clear at the beginning of this little journal, I am not attempting a detailed treatise on the Blessed Sacrament. Still less have I sought to dare a full-blown Catholic apologetic. Rather, my sole aim has been to disentangle one part of ancient orthodoxy from modern error: to invite, not convert. However, it is also obvious where my own investigation has led me: I am an Evangelical who has joined the Roman Catholic Church and whose decision was in part influenced by the discoveries chronicled here. Further, I presume that you, having read this far, also have more than a passing interest, not only in Eucharistic worship, but in Catholic Christianity as a whole. Yet if you are still having difficulties with some of what I have said, I can sympathize entirely. For many years, the thought of "Catholic authority" was, if not unconscionable, at least very abrasive. It entails all sorts of awkward questions. What about Mary? What about purgatory? Or prayers to saints? Or indulgences? What about all that stuff? Still it is worth noting that if the Real Presence itself was once, if you will pardon the pun, hard to swallow, then humility counsels us not to pass swift judgment on these questions either.

So if the Eucharist has whetted your appetite and pricked your conscience but you are still unsure about the Catholic Church, you should be about the business of settling your doubts. This is doubly true since the Church Herself forbids non-Catholics from receiving the Eucharist except under very special circumstances. (Make no mistake. This is not exclusivity, but common sense. After all, you cannot both proclaim your union with the Church [in the Eucharist] while disbelieving in the very foundations of Her authority. Thus, the Catholic Church is simply echoing our own consciences by saying "Don't rush into my arms without a thought. Count the cost.")

That means go slowly. Pray. Investigate. Think. Discern. Most importantly, do not rely on secondary non-Catholic sources as your main guides to "What Catholics Really Believe." (After all, you would not consult the Koran to find out what Christians really believe.) Instead, go to a good catechism or work of

Catholic apologetics and get it straight from the horse's mouth.[69]

A Few Parting Words

In closing, I would like to leave you with three things. First, I wish to stress that, though we should be in formal communion with the Catholic Church to receive the full benefits of the Eucharist, we certainly need no degree in theology. All the fine theological nuances we have discussed above are not the core of the Faith; they are simply machinery for clearing a blocked road. We worship Jesus Christ, not theology. Thus, we need not master a swarm of biblical and philosophical subtleties to receive the Eucharist any more than we need master the blueprints of a microwave oven to eat lunch. As someone said, God has never been terribly impressed with the best ideas, but the offering of a human heart

---

[69]I recommend Dr. Alan Schreck's *Catholic and Christian* (Ann Arbor, MI: Servant Publications, 1984) as an excellent overview of controversial Catholic doctrines. It is concise, readable and very sympathetic to the concerns of faithful Protestants. Dr. Schreck's catechism, *The Basics of the Faith* is excellent as well. Also, Dr. Thomas Howard's *Evangelical Is Not Enough* (see note 26) is, to my mind, one of the very best bridges to the Eucharistic/liturgical church that an Evangelical can take. Additionally, there is a short bibliography at the end of this book.

always makes Him sit up and take notice. The crucial thing is to receive in faith the Body and Blood, and live out the mystery of the Risen Christ. All theology is only to help us achieve this union or it is nothing. "The command, after all, was Take, eat: not Take, understand."[70]

Second, I want to stress that my allegiance to the Catholic faith is in no way a repudiation of my Protestant roots. On the contrary, I will go to my grave recounting the glad and incalculable debt I owe Protestant Christianity. For it was there that I first heard proclaimed the Good News of Jesus Christ; there that He first opened His arms to me when I was on the brink of despair; there that I first experienced the richness of the Blessed Trinity, of Bible-centered teaching and of faithful, Spirit-filled love and fellowship. There too did I acquire a living faith in the supernatural power and reality of the Risen Christ. I will always credit the unblinking, no-nonsense Evangelical attitude to truth and falsehood with giving me my spiritual "immune system." Such an attitude infused into my bones, in a way deeper than words, a profound love for sanity and life even as it taught me an unshakable dread of ersatz religion and shallow philosophies. My Protestant tradition was and is the mother who nurtured me. As Judaism was the taproot of all that the Apostles received

---

[70]C. S. Lewis, *Letters to Malcolm: Chiefly on Prayer* (New York: Harcourt, Brace, Jovanovich, Inc., 1964), p. 104.

from Christ, so are my Evangelical roots for me. And as Christianity is the flower of the faith of Israel, so my Catholic faith is the blossom of all that I love best in Protestantism. Like a Jewish Christian, I do not consider myself converted, but completed.

Finally, as one who has walked a little way down the road, I can say with all honesty that I understand just how hard it is for many faithful Protestant Christians to contemplate these things. Indeed, if I could have done so without compromising the truth, I would have left out the whole business of apostolic authority in relation to the Eucharist. For to call people to experience the pain of a shattered Christendom is to run the risk of summoning up ancient grudges; grudges which may tempt us to further carve up Christ's dismembered body with the knives of accusation and counter-accusation. Such a call invites you into the very real possibility of soul-searching doubt, personal ridicule, temptation to retaliate, difficult and extended study, and alienation from friends and family. My own experience of such pain (which was due in good measure to my own sin) tempted me to downplay to you the crucial importance of the Eucharist even in the teeth of what I knew about it. "Better to let sleeping dogs lie," said the tempter, "than take a chance on opening old wounds. Why don't you just forget about it."

But, as the Parable of the Talents tells us, we neither can nor should forget about it. Nor need we.

For if Christianity is true, fear and pain are not our masters. Indeed, pain itself — the very pain of our doubts and divisions — if offered up to God, will be glorified by Him as a participation in Christ's sufferings. In Him, our struggles may be consecrated and transformed by God into sacraments of His high favor and rich blessing. Therefore, if your heart is troubled by what I have said here, know this: your pain is nothing less than a share in the life of that same crucified and risen One Who, as we have seen, is offered in the Eucharist. And as Paul says, if we share in His sufferings, we will also share in His glory.[71]

---

[71]Romans 8:17.

Suggestions for Further Reading

Eucharist. Louis Bouyer. South Bend, IN: Notre Dame University Press, 1968. *The* expert to consult on further questions pertaining to Holy Communion.

For the Life of the World. Alexander Schmemann. Crestwood, NY: St. Vladimir Press, 1973. According to Thomas Howard, this is "a lucid and compelling explanation, for 'outsiders', of the sacramentalist viewpoint."

Fundamentals of the Faith. Peter Kreeft. San Francisco: Ignatius Press, 1988.

The New Catholics. Dan O'Neill, ed. New York: Crossroad/Continuum, 1988. A wonderful collection of 17 personal encounters with Catholic Christianity. Contributors include John Michael Talbot, Sheldon Vanauken, Dale Vree, and a fascinating collection of people from Evangelical, Seventh Day Adventist, Buddhist, New Age, Anglican, Jewish and atheist backgrounds. Something for everyone here.

The Teaching of Christ: A Catholic Catechism for Adults. Ronald Lawler, Donald W. Wuerl, Thomas Comerford Lawler, eds. Huntington, IN: Our Sunday Visitor, Inc., 1983. Revised Edition. A good, solid catechism.

Vatican Council II: The Conciliar and Post-Conciliar Documents. Austin Flannery, ed. Boston: Daughters of St. Paul, 1988. Revised Edition. Not a book to curl up with on a rainy afternoon, but absolutely indispensable as a reference resource.